COWBOY ED

BY BILL GROSSMAN

ILLUSTRATED BY FLORENCE WINT

A Laura Geringer Book

An Imprint of HarperCollins*Publishers*

Cowboy Ed
Text copyright © 1993 by Bill Grossman
Illustrations copyright © 1993 by Florence Wint
Printed in the U.S.A. All rights reserved.

Library of Congress Cataloging-in-Publication Data
Grossman, Bill.
    Cowboy Ed / by Bill Grossman ; illustrated by Florence Wint.
        p.   cm.
    "A Laura Geringer book."
    Summary: When it starts raining buffalo and bears, some prairie
folk who don't know how to handle this new problem turn to young
Cowboy Ed for help.
    ISBN 0-06-021570-4. — ISBN 0-06-021571-2 (lib. bdg.)
    [1. Frontier and pioneer life—Fiction.   2. Humorous stories.
3. Stories in rhyme.]   I. Wint, Florence, ill.   II. Title.
PZ8.3.G914Co   1993   92-23393
[E]—dc20   CIP
                                                                    AC

Typography by Christine Kettner
1   2   3   4   5   6   7   8   9   10
❖
First Edition

To my brothers and sisters:
Dan, Doug, Barbara, Ellen, and Steve
                              —B.G.

To Doris E. Widerkehr,
                my sister, who has
                always been there
                when I needed her
                              —F.W.

At midnight Cowboy Ed
Went scampering from bed
To the kitchen where,
As often in the past,
He hopped upon his steed,
And rode with blazing speed
To the prairie,
Where the folks were eating grass.

And the horses
Rode the cowboys—
The plows were pulled
By plowboys, and the people
Put their underwear on last.
When Ed inquired why,
He received this strange reply:
"That's the way
We've always done it
In the past."

And the chickens
Stretched their legs
While farmers hatched the eggs,
And the children
Taught their teachers in the class.
Ed asked why that was.
They told him, "It's because
That's the way
We've always done it
In the past."

It started raining bears,
And buffaloes and mares,
And elephants and pigs
And dogs and cats.
The ladies and the fellas
Carried cacti for umbrellas
In the way
They'd always done it
In the past.

But the animals
Kept dropping,
Never pausing,
Never stopping,
And the sea
Of living creatures
Got so vast
That it covered up
The prairie
Which was mighty,
Mighty scary
And had never,
Ever happened
In the past.

There were creatures
All around,
In the bushes,
On the ground,
In the closets,
In the beds,
And in the baths.
Not a single person knew
Quite precisely what to do,
Having never
Faced this problem
In the past.

In the sinks and on the tables
There were minks,
And there were sables.
In the chimneys,
There were beavers and giraffes.
So the people had to do
Something clever, something *new*—
Something no one had attempted
In the past.

Then the mothers
And the daughters
Came out running,
Swinging swatters
They had used
For chasing insects
In the past.
But the zebras
And the otters
Simply gobbled up
The swatters.
And the animals
Remained there
All amassed.

The people left the town
But were feeling
Rather down,
For they hadn't ever left it
In the past.
They decided
They would float
Down the river in a boat,
So they built
A giant schooner
With a mast.

But the schooner never got 'em
Very far—it had no bottom,
For they hadn't ever built one
In the past.
Then the people, looking sickly,
Screamed, "We need a hero quickly!"
They were feeling very
Horribly harassed.

"I'm a hero," shouted Ed.
"And I always use my head.
And I seldom give a hoot
About the past.
I find, when in a pickle,
It is often wise to tickle. . . ."
Something no one would have
Thought of in the past.

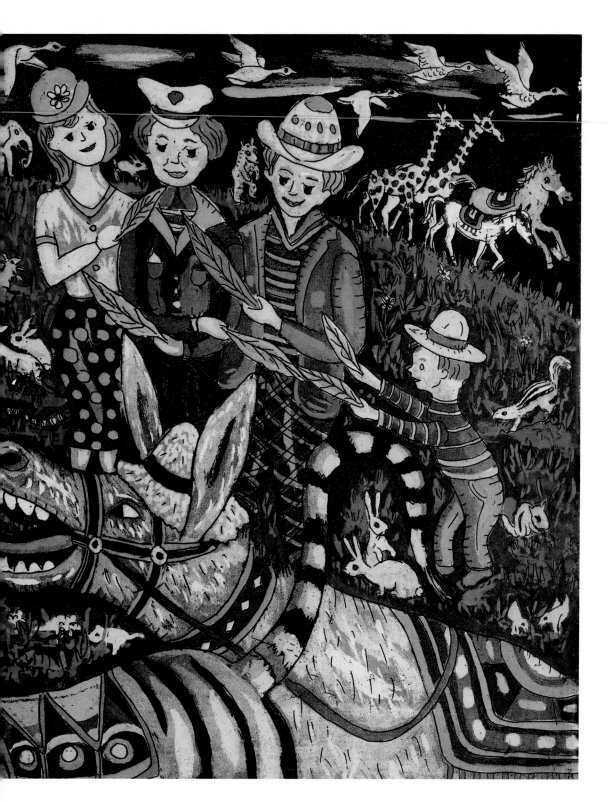

Then he tickled
All the monkeys
And the tigers
And the donkeys,
Who scurried
To the mountains very fast.
He gave the folks
A feather,
And they tickled
All together,
Even though
They'd never done it
In the past.

All the creatures ran away.
Cowboy Ed had saved the day
With his innovative tickling attacks.
The folks had learned from Ed
That it's best to use your head
And to never mind what happened
In the past.

Then Ed fell sound asleep,
And his horse, without a peep,
Went trotting home
With Ed upon his back.
Ed's mother found him snoring
In the kitchen in the morning—
The way she's often found him
In the past.